CHRISTY BOWER

CHOSEN

A 31-Day Christmas Devotional

Chosen: A 31-Day Christmas Devotional

© 2017 Christy Bower

http://christybower.com/

ISBN-13: 978-1981276639

ISBN-10: 1981276637

Greetings

A couple thousand years ago, God chose two young teens to parent the divine child—the promised Messiah of Israel who would claim the throne of David.

Along with that holy calling came all kinds of difficult circumstances. Joseph and Mary experienced shame and disgrace, an unmarried pregnancy, questions, doubts, fears, poverty, and childbirth during travel. They also fled as fugitives and lived as refugees in Egypt to protect Israel's Most Wanted—the holy child, Jesus.

God puts you in challenges that allow him to work through you in amazing ways. Let him meet the challenges of life through you because his burden is light.

May these devotional readings give you hope and courage to face the challenges God has placed in your life. Have a wonderful Christmas!

Christy

December 1

Chosen by God

In the sixth month of Elizabeth's pregnancy, God sent the angel Gabriel to Nazareth, a village in Galilee, to a virgin named Mary. She was engaged to be married to a man named Joseph, a descendant of King David. Gabriel appeared to her and said, "Greetings, favored woman! The Lord is with you!"

Confused and disturbed, Mary tried to think what the angel could mean. "Don't be afraid, Mary," the angel told her, "for you have found favor with God! You will conceive and give birth to a son, and you will name him Jesus. He will be very great and will be called the Son of the Most High. The Lord God will give him the throne of his ancestor David. And he will reign over Israel forever; his Kingdom will never end!"

Mary asked the angel, "But how can this happen? I am a virgin."

The angel replied, "The Holy Spirit will come upon you, and the power of the Most High will overshadow you. So the baby to be born will be holy, and he will be called the Son of God. What's more, your relative Elizabeth has become pregnant in her old age! People used to say she was barren, but she has conceived a son and is now in her sixth month. For the word of God will never fail."

Mary responded, "I am the Lord's servant. May everything you have said about me come true." And then the angel left her.

Luke 1:26-38

Mary was a young teenage girl living with her parents and engaged to marry Joseph. One can imagine she spent her spare time preparing for her marriage and home. An unfamiliar voice interrupted her thoughts. "Greetings, favored woman! The Lord is with you!" The majestic angel stood before her. "Don't be afraid, Mary, for you have found favor with God! You will conceive and give birth to a son, and you will name him Jesus."

I can imagine her stammering in shock. "Um. Ah. I am a virgin. How on earth?" "The Holy Spirit will come upon you, and the baby will be the Son of God."

Mary experienced a wave of confident trust sweep over her. "I am the Lord's servant. May it be."

The angel left her.

Silence.

What just happened? A baby? Me? How? When? What does this mean?

That was a load to drop on a young girl. God believed she was up to the challenge because he chose Mary.

Mary accepted the news with calm acceptance. Whatever God had planned, she was on board with it. No wonder God selected her.

What load has God dropped on you? Are you confused or doubtful? Or are you ready to accept it without question?

Mary didn't know God's whole plan because the angel only told her the sliver of information she needed to understand right now.

Even if you don't comprehend God's purpose in your circumstances, can you accept his lead for this step, right now?

Prayer

Lord, I accept your plan for my life. I can't see the whole picture, but you can. It feels like you have given me some overwhelming challenges and I don't know why, but I will trust you to work out your purposes for my life. I accept my situation. I am on board with whatever you want me to do next, no matter what it might cost me personally. I am your servant, Lord.

December 2

God Chose You

Even before he made the world, God loved us and chose us in Christ to be holy and without fault in his eyes.

Ephesians 1:4

Reflection

God chose you. It's a comforting thought, isn't it? You aren't an accident. Life is not fate. And your faith in Christ is not mere coincidence. The best and worst moments of your life are equally part of God's plan. He chose you to experience these things. Your life experiences are unlike anyone else's experiences. You have the exact qualifications for your role in God's story. When trouble comes, consider it on the job training!

God's plan wasn't thrown together as things came up. No, God chose you before he made the world. That's mind-boggling.

I don't want to give anyone the wrong idea though. God chose everyone, but some people reject God. Their rejection doesn't mean God didn't choose them. It means God chose them and they said, "no."

God chose you for salvation so he could have a relationship with you. He also chose you for a unique role in his story on earth. No one else can fulfill your role because you are unique. No one can express God like you can. We, as Christians, are Christ in the flesh.

Christ is in you and you are in Christ. Union. Two made one. No wonder the Bible uses so many marriage metaphors.

You are in Christ. When God looks at you, he doesn't see your sinful self because you are hidden in Christ. He sees his perfect Son when he looks at you because you are clothed with Christ, "holy and without fault in his eyes."

In addition, Christ is in you. With Christ living in us, we can allow him to live through us, expressing his love and grace to others. You are an incarnation of Christ, God in the flesh, because Christ lives through you. Your hands are his hands, touching lives, serving people, and lifting others up in Christ. That's a high and holy calling.

Prayer

Lord, I'm amazed that I am in Christ and covered by Christ so when you look at me, you see Christ. I am astonished to realize I am an incarnation of Christ on earth. You want to live through me to touch people's lives. These wonderful truths challenge my thinking and elevate my understanding of my relationship with you. Thank you for choosing me.

December 3

Well, That's Awkward

This is how Jesus the Messiah was born. His mother, Mary, was engaged to be married to Joseph. But before the marriage took place, while she was still a virgin, she became pregnant through the power of the Holy Spirit. Joseph, to whom she was engaged, was a righteous man and did not want to disgrace her publicly, so he decided to break the engagement quietly.

Matthew 1:18-19

Reflection

After Mary's visitation from the angel, she rushed to tell Joseph she was pregnant. One can imagine his reaction.

"What? You're kidding me, right?"

"No, Joseph, an angel visited me and told me I will conceive and give birth to the Son of the Most High."

"But I didn't. We haven't. Who is the father if not me?"

"Joseph, I am faithful to you. I promise."

"Well, there has to be a father. That's how you got pregnant. If I find out it was your friend, David."

"Joseph, please. Listen. That's not what happened. Believe me."

Joseph had a difficult time accepting her story. Who wouldn't? The miraculous nature of Mary's conception was . . . inconceivable!

Just as God chose Mary, God chose Joseph. The Son of God needed a stepfather to raise him in the ways of the Lord. Joseph was in an awkward position. Mary claimed to be pregnant. She appeared to have shamed him by being unfaithful and lied to him.

Joseph cared for Mary, but once people discovered Mary's pregnancy, she faced public humiliation and gossip. What could he do to protect his honor and her dignity? He intended to break up with her as quietly as possible so as not to put her to public disgrace. It's easy to see why God selected Joseph.

God selected you, too. Things might appear confusing or even hopeless. Nothing is hopeless in God's plan. He can turn around any circumstances.

God put Joseph in an awkward place but that night God's answers unfolded to Joseph.

If you're dealing with uncomfortable circumstances, lean into God. He will allow you to struggle, but he will show you the way.

Prayer

Lord, I can't do this alone. My life and circumstances don't make sense. You have chosen me for a purpose. I have a role in your story. But what is it? Help me make sense of the rubble in my life because it certainly doesn't feel like a glorious purpose. Give me eyes to see you at work in my life and ears to hear you guiding me along the way.

December 4

Need Wisdom? Just Ask!

Scripture

If you need wisdom, ask our generous God, and he will give it to you. He will not rebuke you for asking.

James 1:5

Reflection

Should I break up with her or not? We each face significant dilemmas and they weigh heavy on us because of the emotions attached to the decisions. We agonize deepest when we care the most. If we didn't care, we'd make a quick decision.

Joseph was engaged to Mary when he found out she was pregnant. And her "story" that it was from God and an angel told her—unbelievable! The Bible is full of events that aren't mere history; they are events from the lives of real people facing the same decisions and emotions we face today. Sure, the lifestyle might be different, but the visceral impact of life events is the same in any generation.

What dilemmas are you facing? Is there a decision on the horizon for you? College? Career? Family? Friends? Travel? Whatever you face, no matter how deeply involved you are or how much it hurts, God is there for you. If you need advice or wisdom, just ask him. He will be glad to give you advice. There's nothing wrong with asking for help. God loves it when we depend on him.

But when you ask for advice, you need to be ready to set aside your preferences and do whatever God tells you. When people say their prayers "hit the ceiling" without a reply, they experience frustration that God isn't answering their prayers. This can happen when we want God to approve our plans without being willing to listen to what he has to say. If you're not interested in listening, God's not going to bother.

If you have a heart that wants whatever God wants for you, ask for wisdom and he will freely give it. The more your relationship with God grows, the more the wisdom from above will naturally flow. God will show you what to do before you even ask!

Prayer

Lord, I come to you today asking for wisdom. There are areas of my life that are not functioning as well as I'd like so I hand them over to you. Please show me what to do in each of these areas. Please make it clear so I understand. I know an angel probably won't appear on my doorstep, but I really want to know what you want me to do and I will do what you tell me, to the best of my ability. Thank you for leading and guiding me. I look forward to your answers and the wisdom I need to live for you.

Whispers. Gossip. Want to Get Away?

Scripture

A few days later Mary hurried to the hill country of Judea, to the town where Zechariah lived. She entered the house and greeted Elizabeth. At the sound of Mary's greeting, Elizabeth's child leaped within her, and Elizabeth was filled with the Holy Spirit.

Elizabeth gave a glad cry and exclaimed to Mary, "God has blessed you above all women, and your child is blessed. Why am I so honored, that the mother of my Lord should visit me? When I heard your greeting, the baby in my womb jumped for joy. You are blessed because you believed that the Lord would do what he said."

Luke 1:39-45

Reflection

It had only been a few days since the angel appeared to Mary. Joseph didn't believe her and was thinking about breaking up. Her parents may not have believed her either. After all, it was an incredible tale—"an angel told me I'm pregnant with the Son of God." Yeah, right.

People may have accused her of making up an incredible lie to cover her misdeed of getting pregnant before marriage. Some may have accused her of blasphemy for bringing God into her cover-up. People around town were beginning to whisper about her. She couldn't help but notice. She needed to get away.

The angel had mentioned her cousin Elizabeth was pregnant after years of barrenness. She would go see her. If Elizabeth was with child, as the angel claimed, it would confirm the whole event. She needed that bit of confirmation because life was falling apart. One day she was happily engaged to be married and the next day everyone was accusing her of misconduct.

We've all felt the sting of other people not believing us. We've experienced the shame of other people gossiping about us. No wonder Mary wanted to get away. Don't we all feel like that at times?

Elizabeth was overjoyed to see Mary. Filled with the Holy Spirit, Elizabeth poured out a loving blessing to Mary that must have soothed and healed Mary's concerns. Elizabeth said the baby in her womb jumped for joy when she heard Mary's greeting.

So it was true. Elizabeth was pregnant, as the angel told her. This confirmed the words of the angel. She, too, must be pregnant, as the angel said.

Girl talk ensued. Elizabeth told the tale of the angel appearing to her husband, Zechariah. He had been speechless ever since. Hearing of someone's angelic visitation assured Mary that her own experience was real. She wasn't going crazy after all.

When Mary arrived, Elizabeth was in her sixth month of pregnancy and Mary stayed for three months, which means she stayed with Elizabeth until the baby was born. They named him John.

Mary did more than run away from her problems and the troublesome responses of her friends and family. She didn't just escape; she sought friendship and comfort. She sought out someone who would understand without judging her. She needed a friend to encourage her when she felt like she was at a breaking point. And she spent her time being productive by helping someone else instead of focusing on herself.

God has chosen you, but that doesn't mean everything will be roses along the way. People may not believe you. They may question your motives. They may even abandon you. But God has chosen you to follow this path and he will work through you to accomplish his purposes. He will also give you the support you need along the way, such as a good friend, a chance to get away for a time, or a period of refreshing before the next hard thing. Look for the blessings God leaves you to refresh you along the way.

Prayer

Lord, I have experienced some of what Mary experienced. Some people haven't believed me or have questioned my motives. Others have broken up our relationship. I've experienced gossip and shame. Sometimes I just want to get away from it all, but I know you have chosen me to walk this path. You have a purpose for my life and a role for me in your story. Give me the support I need. Heal the wounds inflicted by those closest to me. Make my heart glad, even as I endure difficult things. Thank you for being with me, for living in me, and for living through me for your glory.

Amen! Thank-you. You have done great things your daughter, Kathy.

December 6

Chosen to Overcome Shame

Scripture

Therefore, since we are surrounded by such a huge crowd of witnesses to the life of faith, let us strip off every weight that slows us down, especially the sin that so easily trips us up. And let us run with endurance the race God has set before us. We do this by keeping our eyes on Jesus, the champion who initiates and perfects our faith. Because of the joy awaiting him, he endured the cross, disregarding its shame. Now he is seated in the place of honor beside God's throne. Think of all the hostility he endured from sinful people; then you won't become weary and give up.

Hebrews 12:1-3

Reflection

When we think of being chosen by God, we think of grand and glorious things. While God's purpose for us may glorify him, it may not seem so glorious to us at the time. In fact, there's a good chance our purpose may lead us right into conflict.

God chose Mary to carry the Christ-child, a purpose that would glorify God. But she also bore the shame of an unexpected pregnancy, and the further burden of trying to explain she hadn't misbehaved because it was God's child. This explanation would have raised the eyebrows of even the most devout followers of God. When God chose her to fulfill her role in God's story, he also chose her to endure the disgrace that would go along with being misunderstood.

19

According to Hebrews 12, Jesus also experienced shame. Crucifixion was the death of a common criminal. Naked, broken, insulted—Jesus endured both physical pain and the shame of being misunderstood. But Hebrews says Jesus endured the cross and disregarded its shame. How? Because of the joy awaiting him. Beyond this temporary pain and embarrassment is a glorious future in heaven.

We, too, can endure hardship and shame because of the joy ahead of us. Whatever pain we endure is temporary. We can look forward to what lies beyond the pain—if not on earth, then in heaven for all eternity.

In addition, we can experience comfort from God in our hardships (2 Corinthians 1:4-5) because Christ himself experienced the same physical and emotional pain (Hebrews 2:18). He knows and cares. God would never call you to do something without going through it with you. God lives inside you so when we allow him to live through us, our burden is light (Matthew 11:30).

Prayer

Lord, thank you for choosing me to have a role in your story. I know sometimes it will be painful and difficult, but you will always be with me. I know that pain is temporary and your love for me is eternal. Whatever I have to go through now is barely a blip on the radar of eternity. Help me to keep my hardships in perspective. Please teach me to allow you to live your life through me so my burden is light. I look forward to what we can do together.

God Has Done Great Things for Me

Scripture

Mary responded,

"Oh, how my soul praises the Lord. How my spirit rejoices in God my Savior!

For he took notice of his lowly servant girl, and from now on all generations will call me blessed.

For the Mighty One is holy, and he has done great things for me.

He shows mercy from generation to generation to all who fear him.

His mighty arm has done tremendous things! He has scattered the proud and haughty ones.

He has brought down princes from their thrones and exalted the humble.

He has filled the hungry with good things and sent the rich away with empty hands.

He has helped his servant Israel and remembered to be merciful.

For he made this promise to our ancestors, to Abraham and his children forever."

Mary stayed with Elizabeth about three months and then went back to her own home.

Luke 1:46-56

Elizabeth's Spirit-filled greeting caused Mary to break forth in her own verse of praise. It seems as if this is the moment where it all comes together for Mary. Yes, she accepted the message of the angel, but she had encountered resistance from others so it would be natural to waver. Now that she could see Elizabeth's pregnancy, confirming the message of the angel in a tangible way, she was ready to accept the truth of her own special pregnancy.

Mary rejoices and leaves behind any doubts. She humbly thanks the Lord for noticing her, a lowly servant girl and she acknowledges the honor he has given her for generations to come.

While Mary elaborates on the mighty and wonderful things of God, perhaps the most important one is, "He has done great things for me." In her case, a divine pregnancy is definitely "great things" but I think she is also referring to her life up to that point. She could suddenly see God at work in all of it—her godly parents, her national heritage, and Joseph who she hoped would still marry her. All of it came from God. He was there all along, in every detail of life, and all of it led up to this moment.

Can you say, "God has done great things for me"? When you reflect on your life, can you see the hand of God at work, guiding, protecting, and grooming you for where you are now? Even if your present circumstances are challenging, can you see God in the midst of them? You may not know what God is up to, but you can be sure he is working out his plan in your life, even in the difficult parts—*especially* in the difficult parts.

Prayer

Lord, I trust you. I believe you have chosen me to be part of your story. I don't yet understand my role or purpose, but I trust you. When my circumstances seem challenging, at best, I will look for clues you are at work in the midst of the details. But even if I don't see you at work, I will trust you to reveal yourself and your purpose in due time. Give me strength to do the difficult things you have chosen me to do and restore my faith in trusting you when I don't see the big picture. Amen.

December 8

Chosen to Share

Sing about the glory of his name! Tell the world how glorious he is. . . . Come and listen, all you who fear God, and I will tell you what he did for me.

Psalm 66:2, 16

Reflection

Have you ever been to a store and made a smart purchase? It was an incredible deal so you went out rejoicing in your good fortune. Then you made sure to tell others what a good deal you got. Maybe they can get the same deal or maybe you just want to know where to find other good deals. Whatever the case, you can't stop rejoicing and telling other people about your amazing deal.

That's what happens when God does something amazing in your life. God changes you from the inside out and when you realize it, you can't wait to tell people. Maybe God healed you or answered a prayer. Maybe you just met Jesus or someone you love just came to Jesus for the first time. Maybe you know a prodigal who came back, either physically or spiritually. Whatever God has done for you, it gives you great joy that wells up within you and overflows in a way that almost compels you to tell others what God has done for you.

We have the mistaken notion that evangelism is memorizing a bunch of Scriptures and "spiritual laws" or some other formula for convincing people to turn to God. We couldn't be more wrong!

Sharing your testimony is simply telling people what God has done for you. There's no need to convince, coerce, or get complicated. Just sit down at the fast food place and tell the person next to you that God healed your back last week when you tripped on your garden box and the fall realigned things. God works in mysterious ways.

Now that's evangelism. It's getting personal. It's giving God credit. It's irrefutable because no one can say that didn't really happen to you, right? It's foolproof because any fool (each of us) can tell our stories of God at work in our lives.

What if God isn't working in your life that way? Well, that simply means you need to open yourself up to God and ask him to work in your life. And ask God to open the eyes of your heart so you can see the ways he has worked in your life in the past and how he is working in your life right now.

Prayer

Lord, I ask you to open the eyes of my heart so I can see the ways you work in my life. Please show me how to open my heart to you so I can have an intimate, interactive relationship with you that includes answered prayers. Show me what to pray for by showing me what you want to do in my life and the lives of those around me. Continue to change me from the inside out and give me stories of the things you are doing in my life so I can enthusiastically share them with others.

December 9

Wonderful, Difficult Things

Scripture

As he considered this, an angel of the Lord appeared to him in a dream. "Joseph, son of David," the angel said, "do not be afraid to take Mary as your wife. For the child within her was conceived by the Holy Spirit. And she will have a son, and you are to name him Jesus, for he will save his people from their sins."

All of this occurred to fulfill the Lord's message through his prophet:

"Look! The virgin will conceive a child! She will give birth to a son,

and they will call him Immanuel, which means 'God is with us.'"

When Joseph woke up, he did as the angel of the Lord commanded and took Mary as his wife. But he did not have sexual relations with her until her son was born. And Joseph named him Jesus.

Matthew 1:20-25

After Mary told Joseph she was pregnant with the Son of God, Joseph was understandably shaken. He trusted Mary. She had never lied to him before, but this was too much to believe. Was she trying to cover an indiscretion? Was she going crazy? What should he do?

"I'll quietly break up with her. I don't want to subject her to public disgrace if I can avoid it." Then he went to sleep and had a dream.

In the dream, the angel of the Lord said, "Do not be afraid to take Mary as your wife. The child was conceived by the Holy Spirit and is, indeed, the Son of God. You are to name him Jesus. You have been chosen to have a significant role in raising the Son of God, who will save his people from their sins."

Joseph woke up. Mary was right. He had been wrong to doubt her integrity. He did everything the angel of the Lord commanded. In due time, he took Mary to be his wife.

Can you see how the lives of people are intertwined? God chose Mary, but he did not choose her in isolation. Mary's destiny was also tied to the people around her, especially Joseph, so God had to work in their hearts, too.

Do you ever feel out of sync with others? Remember, just as God is working in your heart and life, he's also working in the hearts and lives of others. Not everything will sync precisely, but things will come together in God's time. Sometimes the best thing we can do for those around us is to pray for God's work in their lives because the condition of their hearts affects others. It's a ripple effect.

No matter what kind of difficult situation or relationship tension you might experience, God is working quietly in the hearts and lives of everyone involved. Trust him to change others from the inside out the same way he changes you.

Lord, thank you for the wonderful, difficult things in my life. The way you work things out is wonderful, indescribable even. Please change me from the inside out so I am always ready to see you at work in situations and in the lives of those around me. Please work in the lives of others, too, changing them just as you change me to be more like you. Remind me to be patient with others, knowing they may not have the same growth path that I have experienced. We all grow in different areas at different times. Give me grace to be kind and loving toward all.

December 10

Chosen for Relationship

Scripture

All right then, the Lord himself will give you the sign. Look! The virgin will conceive a child! She will give birth to a son and will call him Immanuel (which means 'God is with us').

Isaiah 7:14

Reflection

Immanuel is a word mostly heard around Christmas time so you may not be familiar with it. Immanuel (sometimes spelled Emmanuel) means "God is with us." It is a fitting name for Jesus as Son of God.

The Lord prophesied through Isaiah that a virgin would conceive a child. She would give birth to Immanuel. Literally, she would give birth to God with us. That's a powerful image. This vulnerable infant is God with us. God took on human form to be with us. How amazing is that?

God chose to come as a baby, the most non-threatening human form. He wanted to be approachable. He wanted to do everything he could to make a relationship possible. Sometimes you'll hear people refer to him as a "personal God" because unlike false gods, our God has a relationship with us. He is Immanuel, God with us.

You were chosen for a relationship with the Creator of the Universe! The only thing standing in the way of that relationship is you. Are you open to God? Do you want to have a growing, intimate relationship with Immanuel?

In the Old Testament, God told his people he would go with them. Then he said he would walk among them. Now, not only is God with us and among us, he is in us!

As Christians, we have Christ living in us. That takes Immanuel, God with us, to a whole new level. Jesus isn't just among us or with us, he is so intimate he's in us.

We are literally the incarnation or embodiment of Christ in this world. He lives his life through us, through our distinct personalities and gifts. That's an intimate relationship and a remarkable privilege.

Whenever you see a reference to Immanuel, don't just think of baby Jesus or Jesus when he was on earth. Think of all the incredible ways God is with you. He chose you for a relationship with him.

Prayer

Lord, thank you for being Immanuel, God with us. Thank you for desiring a relationship with me and for doing everything possible to be approachable and personal. I do want a relationship with you. I struggle to recognize how real you are. Give me a greater awareness of how you are with me. Reveal yourself as Immanuel to me in ways I can understand. Thank you for expanding my understanding of who you are and what you desire to do in my life.

Divine Inconveniences

Scripture

At that time the Roman emperor, Augustus, decreed that a census should be taken throughout the Roman Empire. (This was the first census taken when Quirinius was governor of Syria.) All returned to their own ancestral towns to register for this census. And because Joseph was a descendant of King David, he had to go to Bethlehem in Judea, David's ancient home. He traveled there from the village of Nazareth in Galilee. He took with him Mary, to whom he was engaged, who was now expecting a child.

Luke 2:1-5

Reflection

Why now? We've all said it or felt it before. We have something big happening and something unexpected gets in the way. We get sick. We are called for jury duty. We get a job transfer. Or we get laid off. Why now?

Mary was due to have the most important baby in the history of the world and Governor Quirinius calls for a census! The expecting mother would have to journey from Nazareth to Bethlehem, a distance of 70-80 miles in a straight line, but they would have had to detour around Samaria.

The Jews and Samaritans hated each other so traveling alone through Samaria would risk being attacked by bandits and no one would be willing to help a Jewish couple if they needed help or had to deliver the baby in route. The long way around was probably more like 90-100 miles. A healthy person could do twenty miles a day, but Mary's late term pregnancy would make it much slower, perhaps 7-10 days.

Interruptions to our plans and unexpected circumstances seem like they get in the way of our lives, but they are generally all part of God's plan. Who hasn't been delayed only to find out there was an accident on the route to work at the exact time you would have passed by if you had left on time? God is in the details, even your lost car keys. Instead of getting frustrated, remember to accept God's timing.

Mary and Joseph couldn't have known they *needed* to be in Bethlehem. Long ago, God has spoken through the prophets who foretold the birthplace of the Messiah: Bethlehem. God had a hand in calling for a census. He knew Joseph would have to return to Bethlehem, the City of David, to be counted.

It was inconvenient to have to travel so far (before modern transportation!) right when Mary was due to give birth. They could have felt frustrated and angry. They could have refused to go. But they were willing, submissive, and obedient to the laws of the land and the laws of their God.

How we feel about inconveniences may not change the outcome, but it will change how we feel. We can choose peace or agitation when things don't go as we wish. Trust God to know why the details of a given situation are important.

Prayer

Lord, I ask for your peace right now. I struggle so often when things don't go right for me. When the expectations others have of me seem inconvenient or life circumstances get in the way, I don't always have a good attitude. I can see how you really do orchestrate the details of life in a complex way that includes each person. Thank you for trusting me to have a part of your work and help me to trust you for the details. Give me patience when things go wrong so I can see you at work in the detours of my life. Thank you.

Never Give Up (No One Said It Would Be Easy)

Scripture

That is why we never give up. Though our bodies are dying, our spirits are being renewed every day. For our present troubles are small and won't last very long. Yet they produce for us a glory that vastly outweighs them and will last forever! So we don't look at the troubles we can see now; rather, we fix our gaze on things that cannot be seen. For the things we see now will soon be gone, but the things we cannot see will last forever.

2 Corinthians 4:16-18

Reflection

Murphy's Law says, "Anything that can go wrong, will go wrong." Although that's a very pessimistic view of things, we all feel like that at times.

Mary and Joseph had to travel to Bethlehem at the same time Mary's baby was due. The poor timing might have seemed like Murphy's Law to them but it was out of their control. They had to obey the law to show up in Bethlehem for the census so they would have to trust God to work out the details.

Little did they know God was working out the details to fulfill the prophecies written about the Messiah centuries earlier—prophecies that said the Messiah would be born in Bethlehem: "But you, O Bethlehem Ephrathah, are only a small village among all the people of Judah. Yet a ruler of

Israel, whose origins are in the distant past, will come from you on my behalf" (Micah 5:2).

When things are more difficult than we wish they were, it's easy to forget God is in the details. He is working things out, even if life seems complicated, inconvenient, and difficult.

Paul wrote to the Corinthian church, speaking openly about being "weighed down with troubles" (2 Corinthians 1:6). He explained it this way: "We were crushed and overwhelmed beyond our ability to endure, and we thought we would never live through it. In fact, we expected to die. But as a result, we stopped relying on ourselves and learned to rely only on God, who raises the dead" (2 Corinthians 1:8-9).

Because of their difficult circumstances, Paul and his companions learned to rely on God. We think trusting God ought to come naturally for Christians, but Paul says he learned to rely on God. Sometimes desperate situations force us to rely on God rather than our fierce independence.

Paul also said they never gave up. They realized their troubles were small and wouldn't last very long. The eternal glory ahead of us outweighs any puny problems we face during our time on earth. We can lift our eyes above our circumstances and see the glory of eternity ahead. The glory ahead will last forever, but our troubles are only temporary.

Prayer

Thank you, Lord, for your grace in working out the details of my life. When life feels out of control, remind me you are in control even when life seems inconvenient, complicated, and difficult. Teach me to trust in you so I learn to rely on you and not myself or my circumstances. Help me maintain an eternal perspective. My troubles are temporary, but eternal glory will last forever. Thank you!

December 13

The Messy Details of Life

Scripture

And while they were there, the time came for her baby to be born. She gave birth to her firstborn son. She wrapped him snugly in strips of cloth and laid him in a manger, because there was no lodging available for them.

Luke 2:6-7

Reflection

We tend to glorify the idea of a calling. Being chosen by God seems like a grand purpose, elevating us above the normal circumstances of life. It simply isn't true. This false filter causes us to see the events in our lives with a distorted view. Knowing God called us for a purpose and we are part of God's plan, we assume things will be wonderful and easy. We set ourselves up for devastating disappointment with these false conceptions.

God chose Mary and Joseph to have and raise the Son of God. Angels appeared to them. It seems so grand and glorious. But God never promised them it would be easy. He never gave them false hope in a perfect path.

Mary and Joseph set out for Bethlehem to fulfill their legal obligation appear in person for the census. They undoubtedly knew Mary could give birth any time. It wasn't going to be easy.

Bethlehem was swarming with people who had converged on their ancestral home, the City of David, for the census. The Bethlehem inns were full. People were camping out wherever they could—the town square, the synagogue, and the courtyards of businesses. The swarms of people were like locusts descending on Bethlehem.

In desperation, Joseph must have told an innkeeper, "Please help us. My fiancé is in labor. We need somewhere for her to give birth—somewhere warm and comfortable, with a bit of privacy."

The innkeeper had compassion and led them around back to the stable. He quickly shoveled the horse dung out of a stall and put fresh hay in there for the expecting mother. "I'm sorry. It's the best I can do for you."

"It will be fine," said Mary as Joseph eased her into the fresh hay.

The barn was filthy and smelled like donkeys, horses, cows, and dung. Germs and bacteria (from the animals and dung) would have been a danger to both mother and child in childbirth. It was not where one would hope to give birth to any baby, especially the Son of God.

God chose Mary and Joseph. They still had to work through the difficult, dirty details.

In our own lives, we think God's calling and purpose for our lives means we won't have to deal with unpleasant, difficult details on the way. If God's in it, we reason, God will make it happen easily. But God's calling doesn't mean he will make it easy. It means he has chosen us to be strong enough to work through the details with him.

Prayer

Thank you, Lord, for trusting me with being part of your perfect plan. Please help me to accept that you have chosen me to deal with the difficulties that I'll encounter along the way. I know you are with me and living your life through me so help me relax when I face difficulties, knowing you will work through me to resolve problems and endure hardship. I know fulfilling your calling for me won't be easy, but it will be worth it.

December 14

Focus on Others

Don't be selfish; don't try to impress others. Be humble, thinking of others as better than yourselves. Don't look out only for your own interests, but take an interest in others, too.

You must have the same attitude that Christ Jesus had.

Though he was God, he did not think of equality with God as something to cling to.

Instead, he gave up his divine privileges; he took the humble position of a slave and was born as a human being.

When he appeared in human form, he humbled himself in obedience to God and died a criminal's death on a cross.

Philippians 2:3-8

Reflection

It's almost beyond comprehension for us to think about God becoming a baby, starting as a divine seed in the womb where he lived in darkness for nine months. Then he was forced out of the darkness into the light in a bloody, messy, birth process. When he first opened his eyes, he may have seen a cow or donkey in the stable where he was born. It wasn't a clean place to enter the world, but it would do.

Actually, if the infant Jesus could have spoken, I think he would have said, "It is good," just as he did at the creation of the world.

Jesus was God, but he was willing to set aside those privileges. He accepted the humble form of a human being. While he was in human form, he humbled himself to obey God and subjected himself to a criminal's death.

God chose to be humble rather than lord it over us. He entered the world in a way that was humble.

Just as Christ chose to be humble, he chose you and I to be humble. God doesn't call us to seek great things for ourselves. He doesn't want us to be selfish or try to impress people. Rather, he wants us to think of others as better than ourselves. he wants us to take an interest in others and not be so self-absorbed in our own interests. Basically, he wants us to have the attitude that Christ demonstrated, humility.

Consider ways you can put others first. In what areas are you self-absorbed? In what ways could you set aside your interests and preferences to demonstrate genuine attentiveness to others? See how much of a conversation you can keep focused on the other person. Make a game of it, if it helps you pay attention. Learn to ask about others more and talk about yourself less. We must learn to ask God to help us be humble and put others first.

Prayer

Lord, I have not been very humble in how I spend my time, money, and even how I engage in conversation. Too much of my life focuses on me. Please work through me to reach out to others. I can't seem to do a very good job on my own, so I'm going to have to depend on you to let your love for others flow through me. Let me see people the way you see them. Teach me how to build others up, rather than building my own little empire. Let your love and grace flow through me so there's less of me and a lot more of you when I deal with other people.

December 15

Just Show Up

That night there were shepherds staying in the fields nearby, guarding their flocks of sheep. Suddenly, an angel of the Lord appeared among them, and the radiance of the Lord's glory surrounded them. They were terrified, but the angel reassured them. "Don't be afraid!" he said. "I bring you good news that will bring great joy to all people. The Savior—yes, the Messiah, the Lord—has been born today in Bethlehem, the city of David! And you will recognize him by this sign: You will find a baby wrapped snugly in strips of cloth, lying in a manger."

Suddenly, the angel was joined by a vast host of others— the armies of heaven—praising God and saying,

"Glory to God in highest heaven, and peace on earth to those with whom God is pleased."

When the angels had returned to heaven, the shepherds said to each other, "Let's go to Bethlehem! Let's see this thing that has happened, which the Lord has told us about."

They hurried to the village and found Mary and Joseph. And there was the baby, lying in the manger. After seeing him, the shepherds told everyone what had happened and what the angel had said to them about this child. All who heard the shepherds' story were astonished, but Mary kept all these things in her heart and thought about them often. The shepherds went back to their flocks, glorifying and praising God for all they had heard and seen. It was just as the angel had told them.

Luke 2:8-20

Reflection

The Son of God. The King of Kings. The Messiah. Here was the one who would save the people of Israel. He would claim the throne of David and rule Israel as a sovereign nation for the first time in several centuries, or so they thought. God's plan was much bigger.

You'd think the occasion would call for royal invitations, receiving dignitaries, press releases, social media campaigns, commercials, t-shirts ("Bethlehem Inn" or "I saw Jesus"), and don't forget the selfies with Jesus! Well, maybe not. It would be so different nowadays, though. Still, the Son of God was born and the best the angels could do is tell a few dirty, mangy shepherds?

God doesn't care about publicity. He doesn't do mass marketing. He works one person at a time. One by one, the word will spread. That's how the Great Commission works. That's how the ministry of Christ worked as he healed people. And that's how the arrival of the Messiah worked— one lowly shepherd telling another average citizen in town for the census. All who heard the shepherd's story were astonished.

God chose the shepherds to be part of God's story. They didn't deserve it. No one does. Nevertheless, God chose them and they participated in a holy moment. They interacted with God-in-the-flesh.

When God chooses us to participate in his story, it doesn't mean we're the most qualified, the best prepared, or the most worthy. God chooses to work through our weaknesses to display his strength. He looks for our willingness, an open heart. God does the rest through us.

Like the shepherds, we don't have to have a social media following, an audience, or a platform. We just show up. That's all the shepherds did. They showed up. God invited them to be part of his story and they showed up. Then, in their uncontainable joy, they told everyone they saw.

Lord, thank you for inviting me to participate in your story. Thank you for choosing me to participate in your plan. I don't ask for a major role. It's not about me. But like a humble shepherd, I come as I am to see what you want to show me. I will tell others what I have seen you do. After all, a witness simply tells others what he or she has seen and heard. Give me opportunities to see you at work so I can rejoice and share those moments with others.

December 16

God Chose the Foolish

Scripture

Instead, God chose things the world considers foolish in order to shame those who think they are wise. And he chose things that are powerless to shame those who are powerful. God chose things despised by the world, things counted as nothing at all, and used them to bring to nothing what the world considers important.

1 Corinthians 1:27-28

Reflection

Shepherds were dirty, smelly, and perhaps a little uncouth. That is, they may not have been the most socially acceptable citizens of Bethlehem. Yet as they watched their flocks by night, God saw fit to give the lowly shepherds a spectacular invitation to see the Holy One. Not just one angel, but a heavenly host appeared to the shepherds with the grand announcement of the Savior's birth.

The world may have looked down on shepherds, but not God. He honored them with the announcement of Jesus' birth and Jesus later referred to himself as a shepherd caring for the sheep. That's the way God works. He chooses the despised, foolish, and powerless things to shame those who should know better, those who think they are wise or powerful. God deflates the things the world thinks are important. But the things the world counts as nothing, God elevates.

47

God turns things upside down like this so none of us can boast before God. We can't make ourselves "good enough" for God by right living. God chooses the foolish things of the world because they are most willing to allow God to use them.

God chooses those among us who admit their brokenness. We are flawed, fragile vessels that might seem useless, but God sees our flaws as a beautiful thing. He fills us and uses us to display his power through our lives.

Paul wrote, "We now have this light shining in our hearts, but we ourselves are like fragile clay jars containing this great treasure. This makes it clear that our great power is from God, not from ourselves" (2 Corinthians 4:7). Broken jars seem useless, but God wants to fill our broken lives so others can see God's great power at work. Then they, too, will give glory to God.

Prayer

Lord, my life has been difficult. I bear the wounds of so many painful things. Come; fill my life with your light. Let your love and power shine through my brokenness. May your love and grace ooze all over the people around me. I know I'm messy, Lord, but if you can use my mess, then please make it a beautiful mess for your glory.

December 17

Does It Mean God No Longer Loves Us If...

Scripture

Eight days later, when the baby was circumcised, he was named Jesus, the name given him by the angel even before he was conceived.

Then it was time for their purification offering, as required by the law of Moses after the birth of a child; so his parents took him to Jerusalem to present him to the Lord. The law of the Lord says, "If a woman's first child is a boy, he must be dedicated to the Lord." So they offered the sacrifice required in the law of the Lord—"either a pair of turtledoves or two young pigeons."

Luke 2:21-24

Reflection

Joseph and Mary followed the law by having the baby circumcised on the eighth day. Then, a few days later, they would have dedicated him to the Lord (Exodus 13:2) and made the offering of purification for mother and child. The law required a lamb for the offering, but if the woman was poor, the law allowed her to offer two turtledoves or two young pigeons (Leviticus 12:8). Because Mary offered two young pigeons, we know they were poor.

God chose Mary and Joseph to be the human parents of the Son of God, but God didn't rescue them from experiencing severe poverty. God didn't clear away the obstacles for them, so why should we expect more? We

49

tend to feel entitled to a good life—a satisfying job, a desirable income, a happy relationship, and good health. We aren't entitled to any of these things.

The "health and wealth" preachers have done a grave disservice by misrepresenting God as a Santa in the sky. God does bless us, but not always the way we expect or desire. No doubt, Mary and Joseph felt blessed, despite poverty and hardship.

According to Romans 8:35, 37:

> Can anything ever separate us from Christ's love? Does it mean he no longer loves us if we have trouble or calamity, or are persecuted, or hungry, or destitute, or in danger, or threatened with death? . . . No, despite all these things, overwhelming victory is ours through Christ, who loved us.

Material blessings aren't a sign of divine favor. If you are poor or experiencing difficulties, it doesn't mean God loves you less or you are somehow not pleasing to him.

Just because God chose you, doesn't mean it will be easy. You may not have all the material blessings so coveted in our culture but you have every spiritual blessing in Christ (Ephesians 1:3).

Prayer

Lord, it is a relief to know my circumstances don't reflect how you really feel about me. I don't have to do more and try harder to earn your blessings or approval. Nothing can separate me from your love, not even poverty or calamity. In spite of my circumstances, you still love me and work through my life to achieve victory according to your plan. Thank you for blessing us with these details in the story of Mary and Joseph so we can see examples of your love, which is separate from circumstances. I accept your love and blessings now.

December 18

Why Jesus Became Poor

Scripture

You know the generous grace of our Lord Jesus Christ. Though he was rich, yet for your sakes he became poor, so that by his poverty he could make you rich.

2 Corinthians 8:9

Reflection

Jesus was born into a poor family. Think about that for a moment. Jesus traded all the lavish riches of heaven to become a human infant born in a barn to parents in poverty. What a trade!

He gave up spiritual riches to become poor so through his earthly poverty, he could give us spiritual riches. Wow. That's powerful. The Bible also says he "has blessed us with every spiritual blessing in the heavenly realms because we are united with Christ" (Ephesians 1:3). He became poor so we could become rich. That's love, compassion, and grace all rolled up into one.

Is there a correlation between wealth and faith? Well, being poor does require living by faith more than being rich. That's why the Bible says, "Hasn't God chosen the poor in this world to be rich in faith? Aren't they the ones who will inherit the Kingdom he promised to those who love him?" (James 2:5). It seems as if the poor are given a special measure of faith and blessing from God. Throughout the Bible, God speaks favorably of the poor, as the special object of his concern.

Regardless of your financial condition, consider the ways God has made you rich in spiritual blessings. God has given us *every* spiritual blessing. That's lavish riches. God has blessed you with love, forgiveness, grace, the Holy Spirit living within you, and infinitely more!

The riches of Christ are ours because Jesus was willing to trade away his own spiritual riches and comfort to become a poor human like us. We are forever grateful for his willingness to become poor so we could become rich.

Prayer

Lord, thank you for the riches you have given me in Christ. You have lavished your love on me to the point of overflowing. I can't completely comprehend what you gave up to become a poor baby, but I am grateful for your willingness to come to earth for us.

December 19
Have You Ever Had a Divine Appointment?

Scripture

At that time there was a man in Jerusalem named Simeon. He was righteous and devout and was eagerly waiting for the Messiah to come and rescue Israel. The Holy Spirit was upon him and had revealed to him that he would not die until he had seen the Lord's Messiah. That day the Spirit led him to the Temple. So when Mary and Joseph came to present the baby Jesus to the Lord as the law required, Simeon was there. He took the child in his arms and praised God, saying,

"Sovereign Lord, now let your servant die in peace, as you have promised.

I have seen your salvation, which you have prepared for all people.

He is a light to reveal God to the nations, and he is the glory of your people Israel!"

Jesus' parents were amazed at what was being said about him. Then Simeon blessed them, and he said to Mary, the baby's mother, "This child is destined to cause many in Israel to fall, and many others to rise. He has been sent as a sign from God, but many will oppose him. As a result, the deepest thoughts of many hearts will be revealed. And a sword will pierce your very soul."

Luke 2:25-35

Have you ever had a divine appointment? Have you ever been certain that God orchestrated events to get you in a certain place at a certain time to meet someone, witness something, or participate in God's work in someone's life?

God loves to orchestrate divine appointments. Simeon had been eagerly waiting for the Messiah. The Holy Spirit revealed to him that he would see the Messiah before he died. One day, the Spirit led him to the Temple. It happened to be the day Mary and Joseph brought the baby to the Temple, as the law required. Mere chance? I doubt it. It was a divine appointment.

Simeon saw them with the infant. He took the baby in his arms and praised God for fulfilling his promise. He had indeed lived to see the Messiah.

The Lord chose Simeon to see the salvation the Lord provided for all people. The Lord orchestrated events to make it possible for Simeon to be in the Temple on the same day as Mary and Joseph. When God chooses you, he also makes things happen you couldn't imagine possible.

God has chosen you. He will work on your behalf to orchestrate the details. When you begin to experience these divine appointments, it will increase your faith in God's ability to do what he says he will do. Not only are you chosen, but he will give you the faith you need to see things through.

Prayer

Lord, life seems like chaos sometimes. But from the beginning, you made order out of chaos when you created the world and all that is in it. There are no accidents or coincidences. You orchestrate the details of life to create divine appointments. I give you permission to create divine appointments for me. Let me run into a person who needs a word of encouragement and a prayer. Help me genuinely see people the way you see them. Give me a heart to take advantage of "chance" meetings and help me see them as part of my role in your story.

December 20

Go This Way (Divine Guidance)

Scripture

Your own ears will hear him. Right behind you a voice will say, "This is the way you should go," whether to the right or to the left.

Isaiah 30:21

Reflection

We're all trying to find our way through life. We wonder what we want to be when we grow up. We wonder whom to marry. We wonder which job offer to take. As we look at this meandering path through life, we wonder where it is leading us.

Jesus said, "I am the way, the truth, and the life. No one can come to the Father except through me" (John 14:6). Jesus doesn't just show us the way. He *is* the way. If the path of our life doesn't lead through Christ, it doesn't go anywhere. True guidance only comes from God because he knows the way for us to follow.

Centuries earlier, Isaiah wrote of God's guidance. "Your own ears will hear God." Today, many people, even many Christians, mock the idea of hearing God's voice. The fact is God does speak to us. It may or may not be an audible voice, but we'll definitely hear it in our mind and spirit. According to Isaiah, receiving God's guidance will be like hearing a voice right behind you saying, "Go this way. Turn right. Now turn left." This might sound like GPS instructions, but the point is that God will show you the way to go if you are listening to his voice.

Simeon was in the Temple the day Mary and Joseph came to present the offerings. The Bible says, "That day the Spirit led him to the Temple" (Luke 2:27). This is the leading and guidance offered by God. It is often an inner prompting by God to get us in the right place at the right time.

Jesus said, "My sheep listen to my voice; I know them, and they follow me" (John 10:27). Following Jesus isn't merely blind following. It is relational. We know God and he knows us so we learn to recognize his voice.

You can distinguish the voice of God as clearly as you might recognize your father's voice. You know his voice because you know him so well. It's unmistakable. The same is true with God. When we know God intimately, we recognize his voice. Any believer in Christ can hear God's voice. Learn to listen and silence the voice of doubt.

Prayer

Lord, thank you for guiding me through life. Thank you for showing me which way to go, even if I haven't been clear on hearing from you in the past. I'd like to do better at hearing your voice so I can receive better guidance along the way. I will set aside time to listen to you and develop a relationship with you that involves two-way conversation. Thank you for wanting to have that kind of relationship with me. I'm so amazed at you.

December 21

I've Been Waiting a Long Time for This

Scripture

Anna, a prophet, was also there in the Temple. She was the daughter of Phanuel from the tribe of Asher, and she was very old. Her husband died when they had been married only seven years. Then she lived as a widow to the age of eighty-four. She never left the Temple but stayed there day and night, worshiping God with fasting and prayer. She came along just as Simeon was talking with Mary and Joseph, and she began praising God. She talked about the child to everyone who had been waiting expectantly for God to rescue Jerusalem.

Luke 2:36-38

Reflection

These three verses give us all we know about Anna. She was eighty-four years old and had lived as a widow since she was probably barely twenty years old. Some might think, *What a waste!* But it wasn't a waste of a young woman's life because she turned to God. Anna lived in the Temple, worshipping God for about sixty years.

God chose Anna to be a prophet, which means she spoke words God gave her, including words about the coming Messiah.

Anna had been preparing all her life for this moment. What was her preparation? She stayed close to God day and night, worshiping him with fasting and prayer. Staying close to God is a high calling, one to which we are each called.

It's easier for us, in a way, because we have God living in our hearts. But it's also less tangible to us. Whereas God once lived in the Temple, where people would go to worship, now God lives in the temple of our human bodies. We worship in spirit.

While Simeon was blessing Mary and Joseph in the Temple, Anna came along. She instantly knew. Her spirit resonated with the Spirit of God at seeing the Christ child. She began praising God. The long awaited day had come. The Messiah was here. God had kept his promise.

This was good news. Anna couldn't keep it to herself. From that day on, she told everyone she met about the arrival of the Christ child, the long awaited Messiah who would save them all. Now it was only a matter of time before the child grew to fulfill his destiny. That was news worth sharing because it gave hope to all people. Their days of suffering had a limit now.

Anna's role in God's plan may seem insignificant, but God thought her role was significant enough to include in the Word of God.

God has a significant role for you, too. It may seem insignificant. It may seem like you're waiting for decades for God to work things out, but be patient and focus on what you can do while you are waiting. Anna worshiped God for sixty years. If you seem to be waiting for God's timing, focus on developing a closer relationship with him. That's the most significant thing any of us can do.

Thank you, Lord, for years spent preparing my heart for what you have planned for me in the future. It may seem like I'm waiting and accomplishing nothing, but it is all part of your plan. Remind me to focus on you during my years of waiting so I'm always growing closer to you. Keep my hope in you that one day you'll reveal the opportunities you have for me. Forgive my impatience. I don't want to miss my part in your story.

December 22

My Life Is Worth Nothing
Unless . . .

Scripture

But my life is worth nothing to me unless I use it for finishing the work assigned me by the Lord Jesus—the work of telling others the Good News about the wonderful grace of God.

Acts 20:24

Reflection

I'm sure you've heard of people climbing the corporate ladder, making it in Hollywood, or becoming an all-star athlete only to achieve their wildest dreams and plummet into depression, substance abuse, or loose living. Occasionally someone will reach the top and commit suicide because he or she discovered the only thing at the top was lonely, aching, emptiness. Living for self is an empty pursuit.

Ever since Adam and Eve sinned in the Garden of Eden, people have been making their choices and pursuing happiness apart from God. The most basic sin is the pursuit of self rather than God.

Just as Anna had lived in the Temple for about sixty years telling others about the Messiah, Paul spent his life telling others about the same gracious Savior, Christ our Lord. Paul was a wanted man by the Jewish zealots (as he had once been). His friends pleaded with him not to return to Jerusalem, but he wasn't interested in sparing his life. He was intent on spending his life for Christ. Paul said the Holy Spirit warned him that jail and suffering were in his future, but that wasn't going to stop him from doing the work God chose him to do.

God chose you for a purpose, too. We easily become obsessed with pursuing our own desires and we forget God called us to be part of his story.

We tend to think of the Great Commission, the Lord's command for us to spread the Good News to all people, as a task for missionaries or evangelists. It seems scary and uncomfortable. We may look at it as an undesirable command we must obey.

But, like Anna who joyfully told others to anticipate the coming Messiah, and like Paul who spent his life telling others the Good News about God's grace, we need to realize the sharing comes as a natural overflow of what God is doing in our lives.

When we share answers to prayer, miracles, and other things God is doing in our lives, it isn't drudgery. It's a joy to share what God has done for us day after day. Perhaps we aren't experiencing God's work in our lives because we fixated on ourselves.

In legal terms, a testimony involves telling others what you have seen, heard, and experienced. We simply tell others about our experiences with Christ. It's not our responsibility to convict, coerce, or condemn. We don't need to know a set of principles or Bible verses. We need the joy of the Lord flowing from our hearts with love and grace. Others will be attracted to God in us and want to know more. How easy is that?

Lord, please help me stop focusing on myself. I want to focus on you. I want to experience your answers to prayers, miracles, and other blessings. I will tell others about your work in my life so you get all the credit. I want to tell others about you. Please give me ways to be an open vessel pouring out your love and grace to others.

December 23

Chosen to Investigate

Scripture

Jesus was born in Bethlehem in Judea, during the reign of King Herod. About that time some wise men from eastern lands arrived in Jerusalem, asking, "Where is the newborn king of the Jews? We saw his star as it rose, and we have come to worship him."

King Herod was deeply disturbed when he heard this, as was everyone in Jerusalem. He called a meeting of the leading priests and teachers of religious law and asked, "Where is the Messiah supposed to be born?"

"In Bethlehem in Judea," they said, "for this is what the prophet wrote:

'And you, O Bethlehem in the land of Judah, are not least among the ruling cities of Judah,

for a ruler will come from you who will be the shepherd for my people Israel.'"

Matthew 2:1-6

Reflection

Who were these wise men or magi from the east? Today we would call them scientists. They were astronomers, mathematicians, historians, and perhaps some degree of astrologers or future-tellers. That is, they used all the scientific means available to them to read the signs so they could predict future events such as the rise and fall of kingdoms or the trends in nature (think Farmer's Almanac) such as predicting a drought.

When the wise men saw a new, unusually bright star appear in the sky, they knew it meant something. They wanted to discover its meaning so they put their investigative skills to work. They probably searched documents for references to such an event, but academic inquiry wasn't enough. They had to find out for themselves so they set out on a journey that may have been two years long. They followed the star all the way to Bethlehem.

Somehow they had ascertained enough information and insight to know the star (a star probably indicated a king) represented a newborn (possibly because it was a new star that appeared) king of the Jews (because the star hung over Israel). They came to Jerusalem asking, "Where is the newborn king of the Jews? We saw his rising star and came to worship him."

King Herod feared losing power to a new rising star who might take his throne. Herod summoned the priests and scholars to find out more. This Roman leader had heard the Jews talk about a long awaited Messiah so he asked the Jewish leaders, "Where is the Messiah supposed to be born?"

"In Bethlehem," was their answer.

Both King Herod and the wise men were inquiring for answers. They wanted to find out more about this new King. Like them, we can spend our lives finding out more about Jesus, but our quest is not for more information, but a relational knowing. We aren't limited to knowing the facts in the Bible. We have the privilege of knowing the King of Kings personally.

God may choose you to investigate details. If God gave you a personality that enjoys science and facts, then use your left-brain strengths for God's glory. On the other brain, God may have given you a personality that is more artistic, freestyle, and fun. In that case, use your right-brain strengths for God's glory.

God made you uniquely qualified to do what he has chosen you to do. He will lead you. You may not have a clear star to follow, but he will lead you to where you need to be to fulfill your role in his story.

Prayer

Thank you for leading and guiding me, Lord. Help me identify the ways you lead me each day. Tune my heart to the nudges of your Spirit. Let me not be afraid to ask questions and seek answers, but also let me rest in faith in your nature. I know you will never lead me astray.

December 24

Seeking Jesus

Scripture

And it is impossible to please God without faith. Anyone who wants to come to him must believe that God exists and that he rewards those who sincerely seek him.

Hebrews 11:6

Reflection

Herod met privately with a number of religious scholars. Herod was a Roman so he wasn't familiar with the Jewish Scriptures and traditions: "He called a meeting of the leading priests and teachers of religious law and asked, 'Where is the Messiah supposed to be born?'" (Matthew 2:4). They told Herod the Messiah would come from Bethlehem (according to Micah 5:2).

This began a massive search for the child. Herod wanted the wise men to report to him when they found the child. Fortunately, God warned them to return by a different route. Then Herod had the Roman soldiers kill all babies in the area two years old and younger. Herod was dead serious about seeking Jesus but he was seeking him for all the wrong reasons.

God wants us to seek after him. I like the image used in this verse in Acts: "His purpose was for the nations to seek after God and perhaps feel their way toward him and find him—though he is not far from any one of us" (Acts 17:27). God wants the nations to seek him and feel their way toward him, though he isn't far from any of us. The Bible

71

often speaks of those who do not know Christ as living in darkness. People are groping around in the dark to find God.

Our verse in Hebrews tells us anyone who wants to come to God must believe that he exists and rewards those who sincerely seek him. Herod wasn't sincerely seeking Jesus; he had other motives.

On the eve of Christmas, maybe we should ask ourselves why we are seeking Jesus? Do we want what he can give us? Do we want answers? Do we want to be part of the "team" for our own social standing? Or do we simply want Jesus?

It's impossible to please God without faith. Anything that is not of faith is not of God. Let's receive the faith God gives us to believe and trust him. Without any selfish demands, let's simply seek Jesus and give ourselves to him.

Prayer

Lord, sometimes I feel like I'm groping around in the dark to find you. Open the eyes of my heart so I may see you for who you really are: my King, my Savior, and my Lord! I am thankful for all you do for me, but I worship you for who you are. Thank you for desiring a relationship with me that I may grow in grace and become more like you.

December 25

Chosen to Worship

Scripture

Then Herod called for a private meeting with the wise men, and he learned from them the time when the star first appeared. Then he told them, "Go to Bethlehem and search carefully for the child. And when you find him, come back and tell me so that I can go and worship him, too!"

After this interview the wise men went their way. And the star they had seen in the east guided them to Bethlehem. It went ahead of them and stopped over the place where the child was. When they saw the star, they were filled with joy! They entered the house and saw the child with his mother, Mary, and they bowed down and worshiped him. Then they opened their treasure chests and gave him gifts of gold, frankincense, and myrrh.

When it was time to leave, they returned to their own country by another route, for God had warned them in a dream not to return to Herod.

Matthew 2:7-12

Reflection

In a private meeting with the wise men, King Herod determined when the star first appeared. He wanted to know how old the child was by now. He also instructed them to go find the child and report to him so he could go worship him, too. God knows the difference between true and false worship. Herod didn't want to worship the newborn king; he wanted to destroy the competition. And he was trying to use the wise men to achieve his ends. God knows. That's why God warned the wise men in a dream to return by a different route and not report to Herod.

No matter how difficult your journey in life, God always has a few surprises for you. Imagine having a quiet day with your son when there's a knock at the door. You open the door and several royal dignitaries from faraway lands greet you. They have come to give luxurious gifts to your child. Now that's a surprise!

The wise men offered true worship. This wasn't because they bowed down and gave him gifts. Their worship was true because it came from the heart. They felt genuine awe at the sight of the newborn king with his mother. After all, they had traveled for about two years and miraculously found the One the star had led them to find. The whole experience must have culminated in a great sense of awe and reverence for the divine child and the powers of the universe that led them to him.

God has chosen us to worship. It's not a matter of going through the right motions or singing the right words. True worship is a matter of heartfelt awe. Worship is being awestruck by God. It's having a "wow" rise up spontaneously in our hearts. It's immersing ourselves in God's grace and rejoicing at the miraculous things he does in our lives time after time.

Prayer

Wow, Lord. You are awesome. I can't believe you led the wise men on a cross-country journey for two years and then specifically guided them to the exact home of the Christ child. I trust you to lead and guide me, too, and I will express my awe and devotion at your great wonders and miracles. I open my heart to believe you can and will do miraculous things in my life and through me to others. I'm only beginning to appreciate your wonderful works. You are truly worthy of praise.

December 26

Worship Christ

Therefore, God elevated him to the place of highest honor and gave him the name above all other names, that at the name of Jesus every knee should bow, in heaven and on earth and under the earth, and every tongue declare that Jesus Christ is Lord, to the glory of God the Father.

Philippians 2:9-11

Reflection

Jesus is Lord! Some people don't believe it, but that doesn't change the truth that Jesus is Lord! Jesus humbled himself but God elevated him and now, at the name of Jesus every knee will bow to him. We have a choice. Everyone will bow before Christ someday. Those who believe and love Jesus will bow in worship. Those who don't believe and hate Jesus will bow in submission. Either way, everyone will bow to Jesus.

God gave Jesus the name above all other names. It's a powerful name, as indicated by these examples:

> "There is salvation in no one else! God has given no other name under heaven by which we must be saved" (Acts 4:12).

> "But these are written so that you may continue to believe that Jesus is the Messiah, the Son of God, and that by believing in him you will have life by the power of his name" (John 20:31).

I hope you feel the sense of awe welling up in your spirit. The work of Jesus in coming to earth to purchase our freedom in Christ is powerful, deep, and multi-faceted. It's worth spending some time worshiping him for the amazing love and humility that brought him to earth.

If the hustle of the season has kept you too busy to spend time with God, take time to worship him and reflect on Jesus, the Name above all other Names.

> "Worship Christ as Lord of your life" (1 Peter 3:15).

> "Come, let us worship and bow down. Let us kneel before the Lord our maker" (Psalm 95:6).

> "Worship the Lord with gladness. Come before him, singing with joy" (Psalm 100:2).

Prayer

Lord, you are awesome! You inspire me to the depths of my being. You humbled yourself because of your great love for me and then God lifted you up. All people will bow before you. All of creation bows before you. I lift your name up where it belongs. I exalt you! You are worthy of my praise. You are worthy of my worship. I bow down in awe of you. You are worthy of my trust and complete surrender to you. Your name instills hope and courage in my heart and I find renewed strength in reflecting on your greatness. Thank you, Lord.

December 27

Israel's Most Wanted Fugitive Child

Scripture

After the wise men were gone, an angel of the Lord appeared to Joseph in a dream. "Get up! Flee to Egypt with the child and his mother," the angel said. "Stay there until I tell you to return, because Herod is going to search for the child to kill him."

That night Joseph left for Egypt with the child and Mary, his mother, and they stayed there until Herod's death. This fulfilled what the Lord had spoken through the prophet: "I called my Son out of Egypt."

Herod was furious when he realized that the wise men had outwitted him. He sent soldiers to kill all the boys in and around Bethlehem who were two years old and under, based on the wise men's report of the star's first appearance. Herod's brutal action fulfilled what God had spoken through the prophet Jeremiah:

"A cry was heard in Ramah—weeping and great mourning.

Rachel weeps for her children refusing to be comforted, for they are dead."

Matthew 2:13-18

King Herod was furious. The wise men never returned with a report on the King of the Jews. But based on the information from the wise men about when the star first appeared, Herod decided the child may be up to two years old. He sent orders to the Roman soldiers to kill all the boys in and around Bethlehem who were under two years old. So the Lord warned Joseph in a dream.

An angel of the Lord said, "Get up! Flee to Egypt with the child and his mother. Herod is going to search for the child to kill him so stay in Egypt until I tell you to return." That night Joseph took his family and left for Egypt.

Imagine waking in the night and packing everything you can quickly take so you could leave before dawn. Mary and Joseph didn't have the opportunity to say goodbye to family and friends. They couldn't leave a forwarding address. They had to leave under cover of darkness for the safety of Jesus.

The Son of God began his life on earth as a fugitive.

Once again, Mary and Joseph's role in God's story wasn't easy. Obedience to God's leading will send you on some grand adventures, but it is also difficult and painful at times.

Sometimes our small role is inconvenient, like dropping everything to obey God. It may not always be a life and death situation, but our responsiveness to his leading and our prompt obedience may be necessary for God's plan. We have a glorious purpose by glorifying God in everything we do, even if it means leaving behind all the comforts of home.

Lord, where you lead me I will follow. When you say, "go" I will go. Whatever you ask, we can do together. Thank you for living your life through me to accomplish greater things than I could ever do on my own. Make my life a vessel, pouring out your love to others. And make me a blessing in everything your Spirit prompts me to do.

December 28

Living by Faith

Scripture

It was by faith that Abraham obeyed when God called him to leave home and go to another land that God would give him as his inheritance. He went without knowing where he was going. And even when he reached the land God promised him, he lived there by faith—for he was like a foreigner, living in tents. And so did Isaac and Jacob, who inherited the same promise. Abraham was confidently looking forward to a city with eternal foundations, a city designed and built by God.

It was by faith that even Sarah was able to have a child, though she was barren and was too old. She believed that God would keep his promise. And so a whole nation came from this one man who was as good as dead—a nation with so many people that, like the stars in the sky and the sand on the seashore, there is no way to count them.

All these people died still believing what God had promised them. They did not receive what was promised, but they saw it all from a distance and welcomed it. They agreed that they were foreigners and nomads here on earth.

Hebrews 11:8-13

Reflection

Just as God told Joseph and Mary to leave their homeland, God told Abraham to leave. He didn't say where; he just said he'd show Abraham. Even though he didn't know where he was going, Abraham obeyed. He didn't need all the facts laid out beforehand. He simply obeyed God. Abraham lived by faith that God would keep his promises.

When God promised Abraham he would be the father of many nations, Abraham believed him. Decades later, Abraham and his wife were still childless and barren, and now in old age. Others might have given up and said God had failed them but Abraham remained faithful.

God did make a great nation from Abraham, but not during Abraham's lifetime. Abraham could see beyond his limited life. He understood that God works things out. Abraham died still believing God's promises because even though he didn't see God's promise come true in his lifetime, he knew it would come true eventually.

We tend to struggle with faith. If we don't see all the facts laid out ahead of time or don't see the results in a timely manner, we lose faith. It's easy to think God has failed us, but God cannot fail. It's our limited perspective that has failed us.

Hebrews 11:1 says, "Faith shows the reality of what we hope for; it is the evidence of things we cannot see." Even if we don't see the evidence, we can have faith that God is faithful and his promises are true. Like Abraham, we can die in faith believing. God will make it so, even if it is after we depart this world.

Prayer

Thank you, Lord, for the examples of faith in the Bible. I need the encouragement of seeing other people struggle and finally "get it" in their relationship with you. Please continue to lead and guide me, even if I don't know where I'm going. I will trust you. When your promises don't seem to be true for me, I will not give up. I would rather die in faith believing they will come true after I'm gone. Help me to live by faith in you.

December 29

Life Is Full of Detours

Scripture

When Herod died, an angel of the Lord appeared in a dream to Joseph in Egypt. "Get up!" the angel said. "Take the child and his mother back to the land of Israel, because those who were trying to kill the child are dead."

So Joseph got up and returned to the land of Israel with Jesus and his mother. But when he learned that the new ruler of Judea was Herod's son Archelaus, he was afraid to go there. Then, after being warned in a dream, he left for the region of Galilee. So the family went and lived in a town called Nazareth. This fulfilled what the prophets had said: "He will be called a Nazarene."

Matthew 2:19-23

Reflection

No one wants to be a refugee. We certainly don't choose that role for ourselves. But when God chose Mary and Joseph to raise the Christ child, their role in God's story led them to become refugees for a time. The angel had warned them to flee to Egypt by night so they did. Some scholars say they spent two years in Egypt.

Once again, the angel of the Lord appeared to Joseph in a dream. He instructed Joseph to return to Israel and assured him the danger was gone. Herod was dead and no one was trying to kill Jesus now.

As they returned to Israel, Joseph learned that Herod's son was the new ruler so in an abundance of caution, Joseph did not return to Bethlehem, where the danger had been. Instead, he took the family to Nazareth.

Life is full of detours. Some of them are disappointing and some are delightful. Detours are God's way of getting us to where we need to be. Sometimes that might even include something as undesirable as being a refugee in a foreign land for a time.

If you feel like you're wasting time in a detour or doing time as some sort of refugee, be assured that God doesn't see it the way you see it. Be patient and make the best of it because God has reasons we can't see.

God has chosen you for a role in his story and getting there may not be a straight line. It rarely is. Expect some detours and crummy roles as refugees, unemployed, or whatever. It's all part of the plan. God never said it would be easy, but it will be worth it in the end.

Prayer

Lord, I want a bigger role, but you want to humble me by making me do time in detours and small roles. Open my eyes to the purpose in the wandering periods of my life. Give me hope for restoration and show me when you're ready for me to get up and move into the next phase. I will follow you anywhere, Lord. Thank you for blessing me and giving me fresh insight into your story and my role in it.

God Speaks in Dreams

Scripture

He speaks in dreams, in visions of the night, when deep sleep falls on people as they lie in their beds.

Job 33:15

Reflection

Have you ever paused to consider the number of times dreams were involved in the birth of Christ? According to the Bible, God used at least five dreams regarding the events of the birth of Christ:

- An angel of the Lord appeared to Joseph in a dream to tell him Mary's child was conceived by the Holy Spirit (Matthew 1:20).
- God warned the wise men in a dream not to return to Herod (Matthew 2:12).
- After the wise men left, an angel of the Lord appeared to Joseph in a dream telling him to flee to Egypt and stay there (Matthew 2:13).
- An angel of the Lord appeared to Joseph in a dream in Egypt to tell him Herod had died and it was safe to return home (Matthew 2:19).
- Joseph learned the new ruler of Judea was Herod's son. God warned Joseph in a dream, so he left for Galilee instead (Matthew 2:22).

One of the five dreams was for the wise men, but the other four were dreams God gave Joseph. God communicated to Joseph through dreams and Joseph understood the dreams as communication from God.

Our culture of rationalism dismisses dreams as our mind unwinding or the after-effects of something we ate. I was taught that dreams were meaningless. But as I inspected the Bible further, I realized there were so many dreams in the Bible, it couldn't be meaningless. And if God is the same yesterday, today, and forever (Hebrews 13:8), then He still communicates that way. God doesn't change.

In fact, God said after He poured out the Holy Spirit (Acts 2), He would communicate through dreams more, not less: "I will pour out my Spirit upon all people. Your sons and daughters will prophesy. Your old men will dream dreams, and your young men will see visions" (Joel 2:28).

God gives us dreams, but He also wants us to understand them so we can act on them as Joseph and others did. Who can interpret dreams?

The Joseph of Genesis was a dreamer. When Pharaoh asked him to interpret a dream, Joseph replied, "It is beyond my power to do this. . . . But God can tell you what it means and set you at ease" (Genesis 41:16).

Another example is Daniel. When the king wanted Daniel to interpret his dream, Daniel replied, "it is not because I am wiser than anyone else that I know the secret of your dream, but because God wants you to understand what was in your heart" (Daniel 2:30).

When you have a dream, ask God what it means and he will tell you. Don't write off God's messages as day-old leftovers from the fridge.

Prayer

Lord, I believe dreams are from you. I want to start understanding what you tell me in my dreams. Give me the ability to recall my dreams so I can wake up and ask you to interpret them for me. Thank you for this fascinating way of communicating with my spirit while I sleep.

December 31

He Will Come Again

Scripture

So also Christ was offered once for all time as a sacrifice to take away the sins of many people. He will come again, not to deal with our sins, but to bring salvation to all who are eagerly waiting for him.

Hebrews 9:28

Reflection

Advent means "arrival or coming." Some Christians refer to the Christmas season as Advent because it celebrates the arrival of Christ. Long before Christ came, the prophets of God foretold of the coming Messiah. Jesus fulfilled these prophecies in amazing detail.

The Bible also foretells the Second Advent or arrival of Christ. Because God kept his promises regarding every detail of Christ's advent, we have strong assurance he will keep his promises regarding the Second Advent.

The first time Christ came to deal with our sin by sacrificing himself on our behalf. By his death and resurrection, he broke the power of sin and death so we could live free by his love and grace.

The second time Christ comes, according to the Bible, he will not be dealing with our sins, but bringing salvation to all who are waiting for him.

Even though God chose us to do hard things, we have our hope set on the return of Christ who will free us from the hardships of our human lives. No matter what life holds for us, God's promise is sure. That's why "we look forward with hope to that wonderful day when the glory of our great God and Savior, Jesus Christ, will be revealed" (Titus 2:13).

All of our Christmas celebrations will pale in comparison to the celebration we have at the return of Christ.

Prayer

Lord, thank you for sending Jesus to fulfill your promises. Remind me to keep my hope on the return of Christ so I don't grow weary of the struggles I face. When I am discouraged at life's difficulties, give me a glimpse of the glory of Christ's Second Advent. Thank you for reminding me of this wonderful promise.

Thank You for Reading

Dear Friends,

Thank you for reading this book. I hope it brought you closer to God this holiday season. My prayer for you is that God would make his home in your heart by faith and that his love, grace, and power would work through you in wonderful ways.

May you find rest and peace in letting God live his life through you. And may you discover new blessings from God each day.

Could I ask a favor? If you enjoyed this book, would you take a moment to rate it on the site where you purchased it?

Christy

P.S. Stay in Touch

I invite you to join my Friend List. I send emails approximately twice a month.

http://christybower.com/email/

About Christy

I enjoy Christmas in Montana. Small towns still celebrate Christmas with parades, carnivals, street festivals, and even yetis. Plus, there's snow! Lots of snow!

Take a walk on a snowy day and you'll notice how quiet things are. The snow muffles sounds and everything seems still and silent.

Although there are plenty of wonderful things to do in Montana, such as hiking, snowshoeing, and skiing if you're so inclined (I'm not), the thing I like best is the slower pace of life. It's quite common to see a handwritten sign on a business window reading, "Gone skiing. Back tomorrow."

I like the idea of being snowed in for the winter. The slower pace of life here gives me time to write.

Christmas Crossword Puzzles

CHRISTY BOWER
CROSSWORD
BIBLE STUDIES
The Birth of Jesus
King James Version

Books by Christy

Crossword Bible Studies

- The Birth of Jesus
- Genesis
- Top 40 Classic Songs in Psalms
- Daily Proverbs
- Books of the Old Testament
- Books of the New Testament
- Matthew
- Mark
- Luke
- John
- Acts
- Romans
- First and Second Corinthians
- Galatians to Colossians
- First Thessalonians to Philemon
- Hebrews and James
- First Peter to Jude
- Revelation

Barefoot Devotions

Unstuck

Sweeter Than Chocolate

Bible Surveyor Handbook

Best Friends with God

Devotion Explosion

The Legend of Dragon Hollow

The Secret of the Sword

The Rise of the Dragon King

You Might Like

Manufactured by Amazon.ca
Bolton, ON

31675915R00052